THE ULTIMATE
air fryer
HANDBOOK

Make way and make room (on your counter) for your new favorite appliance. Everyone loves fried food, but no one wants to eat too much of it as our culture becomes ever more health conscious. Luckily, the air fryer gives you all the crispy, crunchy goodness of a fried, comforting meal without the actual frying. That means less fat, less calories, less mess and less sweating in your kitchen over that scalding pan of oil. In the following pages, we explain everything you need to know about air frying your way to a tastier, healthier diet, and provide more than 60 recipes for you to get started!

4
What is an
Air Fryer Anyway?

8
The Official Case
for Air Fryers

10
Starters
& Sides

32
Snacks & Small Bites

48
Main Courses

76
Comfort Classics

90
Desserts

Cover: Shutterstock

What is an Air Fryer Anyway?

IT'S TIME FOR A BRIEF JOURNEY INTO AIR FRYER 101.

What's It Doing to My Food?

Put very simply, your air fryer is a convection oven specially shaped to mimic the effects of frying. With some cleverly applied hot air, it recreates the crispy feel of fried food without the mess or the added fat. Your food is held in the fryer basket, where the fan moves hot air at high speeds around it. This creates perfectly textured foods like fries, chicken nuggets, onion rings, hot wings and much more. While a traditional oven slowly heats up and then slowly disperses that heat to your food, an air fryer uses rapid air flow to heat up much faster, preventing the soggy fries and burned-on-one-side apps that sometimes come from a traditional oven. The speed at which the heated air moves also helps remove messy mediums like oil. Best of all, because you're not required to add loads of oil, air frying is just as healthy as baking, but much more delicious.

What Can I Make With It? Also What Can't I Make With it?

Air fryers can be used to cook a wide range of meals and

THE ULTIMATE AIR FRYER HANDBOOK

What Is An Air Fryer Anyway?

treats. With a few exceptions, anything you can bake in an oven you can whip up in an air fryer. There are great recipes for everything from chocolate chip cookies to baked cinnamon apples that will highlight your air fryer's versatility. But where the appliance really shines is with making foods that we tend to think of as denizens of the deep fryer. Fries, onion rings, mozzarella sticks, egg rolls and spring rolls, fried pickles, chicken legs and wings and all your favorite treats become guilt free in the air fryer without sacrificing taste or texture. As an added bonus, the air fryer works just as well on those frozen Ore-Ida fries as it does on ones you made from scratch, and no one will ever know the difference. What the air fryer can't do is cook from liquid batter unless you freeze that batter first. It's also not the best medium for cooking fresh veggies or cheese. Most air fryers are also pretty small so they can be conveniently stowed, but that means you might have to cook in batches if you're feeding a lot of people at once.

Why Do I Need Another Gadget In My Kitchen?

We know: cabinet space is at a premium in the kitchen and air fryers are about the size of a bread box. It's also an investment of $100+ dollars unless you're lucky enough to find a sale, which is no small amount for something you just heard of. It is, however, an investment of space and cash worth making if, like many Americans, you're trying to cut down on the amount of fried food you eat. The air fryer's ability to perfectly impersonate deep fried texture will make it easier for you to eliminate the real deal. If you use a lot of frozen snacks and sides, the air fryer is by far the best medium to use, both quicker and tastier than the same dish in a conventional oven. And best of all in the summer months, the air fryer doesn't heat up your kitchen (or whole place) every time you use it.

The Official Case for Air Fryers

BOBBY DJAVAHERI, PRESIDENT OF YEDI HOUSEWARE APPLIANCES, BRIEFLY EXPLAINS WHY HE'S A TRUE BELIEVER IN THE AIR FRYER AND WHY YOU SHOULD ADD IT TO YOUR ARSENAL.

There are all kinds of ways to prepare your food while cutting down on the amount of extra oil and other fattening fillers that you use. An air fryer, however, is the only one that allows you to keep the same treats on your plate while you eschew the fryer. That's why Bobby Djavaheri thinks everyone should own one.

How did you become aware of air frying?
I first used an air fryer a few years back. I think I ordered it off the television. It made some amazing chicken tenders and I was hooked. The machine eventually broke down on me, so being part of a family business and taking pride in our brand, Yedi Houseware, we decided to make our own series of air fryers!

What made you think others would feel as you did about the appliance?
Air fryers are beneficial for those in health conscious households, who are using very little oil. Even more, those young professional couples, who work and have children, are coming home and need to whip something up fast. I love the little prep needed to make food. Within minutes of prepping ingredients, you can place your food in the air fryer and dinner is ready in less than 45 minutes! Plus, with all the accessories included, and cheat sheets for how to use the Yedi Air Fryer, the benefits are enormous for any household.

What are your personal favorites to prepare in the fryer?
I love french fries in the air fryer! And of course, chicken tenders, pizza and steak are super delicious!

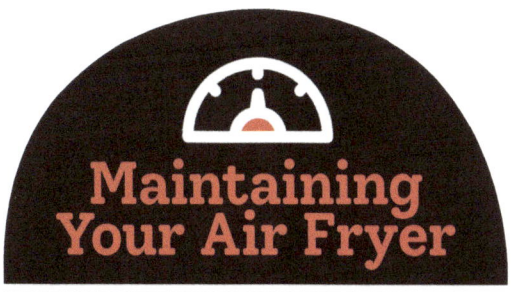

Maintaining Your Air Fryer

All of the components of your air fryer are dishwasher safe, so remove them and wash separately. Sometimes, food matter can get stuck to the heating elements inside the main body of the heater. These can be removed with a brush.

starters & sides

These small plates are guaranteed to elevate your party, guilt-free.

French Fries
Recipe on page 18

Starters & Sides

DIY Tortilla Chips

10 MINUTES » MAKES 1 SERVING

AFTER YOU LEARN HOW TO MAKE YOUR OWN, YOU'LL NEVER GO BACK TO THE BIG BAG O' CHIPS AGAIN.

2 6-inch corn tortillas
1 tsp olive oil
Seasoning of choice

1. Preheat air fryer at 350 degrees F.
2. Slice tortillas into quarters.
3. Brush pieces lightly with olive oil and sprinkle with seasoning.
4. Transfer pieces into air fryer basket and fry for 8 minutes or until crisp.

Tips & Tricks

To get your foods to maximum crispiness, you can give them a quick spray of oil about halfway through cooking.

THE ULTIMATE AIR FRYER HANDBOOK

Starters & Sides

Garlic Parsley Parm Potatoes

20 MINUTES » MAKES 6 SERVINGS

YOU AND YOURS WILL LOVE TUCKING INTO THIS DISH ALMOST AS MUCH AS YOU LOVE TRYING TO SAY ITS NAME FIVE TIMES FAST.

1.5 lbs red potatoes
3 Tbsp olive oil
¼ cup grated Parmesan cheese
2 tsp basil
2 tsp Italian seasoning
2 tsp salt
1 tsp pepper
5 tsp minced garlic

1. Cut the red potatoes in half, and then in quarters, so they end up roughly the same size.
2. In a large mixing bowl, mix everything together in with the potatoes, making sure you coat the potatoes.
3. Pour them into the air fryer basket. Set the time for 10 minutes and the temperature at 390 degrees F.
4. When the first 10 minutes are up, flip the potatoes, and set the time for another 8 minutes.
5. Serve with a sprinkle of fresh rosemary. Plate, serve and enjoy!

Mashed Potato Cakes

25 MINUTES » MAKES 5 SERVINGS

WHY SETTLE FOR THE SAME OLD MASH WHEN YOU CAN FRY UP A NEW FAVORITE?

2 cups mashed potatoes
2 cups flour, sifted
1 cup shredded cheddar cheese
2 tsp salt
3 tsp baking powder
1 tsp garlic powder
1 tsp dried basil
4 eggs, beaten
½ cup milk
1 cup breadcrumbs

1. Combine potatoes, sifted flour, cheese, salt, baking powder, garlic powder and basil.
2. Mix together the eggs and milk and stir lightly into the potato mixture.
3. Form into 4- to 5-inch cakes about an inch thick.
4. Put breadcrumbs in a flat bottom bowl and press both sides of the potato cakes into the crumbs.
5. Place cakes in the air fryer basket. You should be able to fit 3 or 4 at a time.
6. Mist with a bit of olive oil and close fryer.
7. Bake at 400 degrees F for 10 minutes. Turn after 5 minutes and mist with olive oil and finish for an additional 5 minutes.
8. Serve with sour cream, cheese, chives or your favorite garnish.

Starters & Sides

AvoKeto Fries

20 MINUTES » MAKES 2 SERVINGS
AVOCADO REPLACES POTATOES FOR A KETO DIETER'S DREAM, PACKED WITH GOOD FATS.

½ cup (about 2 ⅛ oz.) all-purpose flour
1 ½ tsp black pepper
2 large eggs
1 Tbsp water
½ cup panko (Japanese-style breadcrumbs)
2 avocados, cut into 8 wedges each
Cooking spray
¼ tsp kosher salt
¼ cup no-salt-added ketchup
2 Tbsp canola mayonnaise
1 Tbsp apple cider vinegar
1 Tbsp Sriracha chili sauce

1. Stir together flour and pepper in a shallow dish. Lightly beat eggs and water in a second shallow dish. Place panko in a third shallow dish. Dredge avocado wedges in flour, shaking off excess. Dip in egg mixture, allowing any excess to drip off. Dredge in panko, pressing to adhere.
2. Coat avocado wedges well with cooking spray.
3. Place avocado wedges in the air fryer basket, and cook at 400 degrees F until golden, 7 to 8 minutes, turning avocado wedges over halfway through cooking. Remove from air fryer; sprinkle with salt.
4. While avocado wedges cook, whisk together ketchup, mayonnaise, vinegar and Sriracha in a small bowl. To serve, place 4 avocado fries on each plate with 2 Tbsp sauce.

Starters & Sides

Air-Crispy French Fries

50 MINUTES » MAKES 3 SERVINGS

PAIR THESE PERFECT SPUDS WITH YOUR FAVORITE SANDWICH (OR JUST GRAB A HANDFUL, NO JUDGMENT).

2 Russet potatoes
1 Tbsp olive oil
1 Tbsp sea salt
½ tsp black pepper

1. Blanch the potatoes in water until tender.
2. Let cool. Cut into fries.
3. Toss with olive oil, salt and pepper.
4. Place the potatoes into the fry basket and then into the air fryer.
5. Scroll to the French Fries setting.
6. Adjust cooking time to 18 minutes at 400 degrees F. You might want to cook in two batches for maximum crispiness.
7. Halfway through cooking, shake the fries.

Tips & Tricks

About 2 Tbsp of water in the bottom of your fry basket will keep the appliance from producing small amounts of smoke while cooking greasy foods.

Corn Zucchini Fritters

35 MINUTES » MAKES 3 SERVINGS

MANY A PLATE HAS BEEN BETTERED BY THE PRESENCE OF THE HUMBLE FRITTER: YOURS IS NEXT.

2 medium zucchinis
1 medium potato, cooked
1 cup corn kernels
2 Tbsp chickpea flour
2-3 garlic cloves, finely minced
Salt and pepper
1-2 tsp olive oil

For Serving:
Ketchup or yogurt tahini sauce

1. Grate zucchini using a grater or food processor. In a mixing bowl, mix grated zucchini with little salt and leave for 10 to 15 minutes. Then squeeze out excess water from the zucchini using clean hands or using a cheesecloth.
2. Grate or mash the cooked potato.
3. Combine zucchini, potato, corn, chickpea flour, garlic, salt and pepper in a mixing bowl.
4. Roughly take 2 Tbsp batter, shape into a patty and place on parchment paper.
5. Lightly brush oil on the surface of each fritter. Preheat air fryer to 360 degrees F.
6. Place the fritters on the preheated air fryer mesh without touching each other. Cook them for 8 minutes.
7. Turn the fritters and cook for another 3 to 4 minutes or until well done or until you get the desired color.
8. Serve warm with ketchup or yogurt tahini sauce.

Starters & Sides

Crispy Loaded Potatoes

25 MINUTES » MAKES 4 SERVINGS

THIS IS NOT YOUR MOMMA'S BAKED POTATO, BUT IT IS THE NEW FAMILY STANDARD.

11 oz baby yukon gold potatoes (about eight 2-inch potatoes)
1 tsp olive oil
2 center-cut bacon slices
1 ½ Tbsp chopped fresh chives
½ oz finely shredded reduced-fat cheddar cheese (about 2 Tbsp)
2 Tbsp reduced-fat sour cream
⅛ tsp kosher salt

1. Toss potatoes with oil to coat. Place potatoes in the air fryer basket and cook at 350 degrees F until fork tender, 25 minutes, stirring potatoes occasionally.
2. Meanwhile, cook bacon in a medium skillet over medium heat until crispy, about 7 minutes. Remove bacon from pan; crumble. Place potatoes on a serving platter; lightly crush potatoes to split. Drizzle with bacon drippings. Top with chives, cheese, sour cream, salt and crumbled bacon.

Toasty Garlic Bread

20 MINUTES » MAKES 4 SERVINGS

CALLING ALL COMFORT FOOD LOVERS: THIS CHEESY CLASSIC HAS NEVER BEEN EASIER.

1 lb frozen pizza dough
1 Tbsp garlic
1 tsp sea salt
1 Tbsp fresh parsley, chopped
1 Tbsp Parmesan cheese, grated
½ cup olive oil
Marinara sauce

1. Roll the pizza dough out until ½-inch thick.
2. Slice the dough lengthwise, about ¾-inch apart.
3. Roll the dough between your palm and countertop. Make a knot with the dough and repeat until all the dough is used.
4. Add the spices, cheese and olive oil into a bowl and mix well.
5. Roll the knots into the oil mixture and place into the fry basket. Place into the air fryer.
6. Scroll to the Chicken setting.
7. Set cooking time to 12 minutes at 360 degrees F.
8. Flip over halfway through.
9. Serve with marinara sauce.

Starters & Sides

Aristocrat's Mac & Cheese

60 MINUTES » MAKES 2 SERVINGS

FEELING A LITTLE TOO GOURMET FOR OUR CLASSIC CHEDDAR CONCOCTION (PG. 86)? THIS WILL KICK YOU RIGHT IN YOUR FANCY PANTS.

2 Tbsp, plus ½ tsp salt
½ pound elbow pasta, or your favorite pasta shape
½ cup whole milk
½ cup heavy cream
½ cup grated Fontina cheese
½ cup grated Gruyere cheese
½ cup grated sharp cheddar cheese
½ tsp Emeril's Original Essence
¼ tsp ground black pepper
⅛ tsp ground nutmeg
¼ cup breadcrumbs
¼ cup finely grated Parmesan cheese
1 Tbsp unsalted butter, melted

1. Fill a large saucepan three-quarters full of water and bring to a boil over high heat.
2. Once boiling, add 2 Tbsp salt to the water and then the pasta.
3. Cook the pasta until just al dente.
4. Remove from the water, drain well and place in a medium bowl.
5. Add the milk, heavy cream, Fontina, Gruyere, cheddar, Essence, remaining ½ tsp salt, black pepper and nutmeg and stir well to combine.
6. Place the pasta into the deep casserole pan, and in a separate small bowl, combine the breadcrumbs, Parmesan cheese and butter and stir to blend. Sprinkle over the top of the pasta and place in the basket of the air fryer and close the drawer. Set the temperature to 350 degrees F and the timer for 30 minutes. When the timer goes off, remove the deep casserole pan and allow the Mac & cheese to cool for at least 20 minutes before inverting the deep casserole pan over a plate and removing the pan to release the mac & cheese. Cut into wedges and serve warm.

Starters & Sides

Air-Roasted Corn

20 MINUTES » MAKES 4 SERVINGS

NATURE'S FAVORITE DELIVERY SYSTEM FOR SALT, PEPPER AND BUTTER JUST GOT A MAKEOVER THANKS TO YOUR AIR FRYER.

4 fresh ears of corn
2 to 3 tsp vegetable oil
Salt and pepper to taste

1. Remove husks from corn, wash and pat dry. You may need to cut the corn to fit in your basket.
2. Drizzle vegetable oil over the corn, working to cover the corn well with the vegetable oil.
3. Season with salt and pepper. Cook at 400 degrees F for about 10 minutes.

Potato Skins

40 MINUTES » MAKES 5 SERVINGS

OH, WE'RE SORRY, ARE YOU STILL OVEN-BAKING YOUR POTATO SKINS? WELL THEN ALLOW US TO RETORT.

5-10 small baking potatoes, baked ahead of time
½ cup shredded cheddar cheese
½ cup crumbled bacon
Thinly sliced chives
Dean's Bacon Cheddar Dip

1. Season the outside of potatoes with a drizzle of oil and your favorite spices.
2. Bake potatoes ahead of time in your oven.
3. Once the potatoes are done and cool enough to handle, slice each one in half.
4. Scoop out most of the flesh from the inside of the potato. Be sure to leave a good amount around the edges.
5. Sprinkle each half with cheddar cheese and bacon crumbles.
6. Place them in your air fryer. Cook for 5 to 7 minutes or until the cheese is melted.
7. Transfer them to a plate and top with chives and french onion dip.

Tips & Tricks

When cooking food items that have to be removed from the fryer at a certain temperature, a quick-read thermometer is an investment that will save you some time and headaches.

THE ULTIMATE AIR FRYER HANDBOOK

Starters & Sides

Sage & Onion Stuffing Balls

20 MINUTES » MAKES 2 SERVINGS
NEED A QUICK DOSE OF THANKSGIVING? THESE DELICIOUS POPABLES WILL PUT YOU IN THE HOLIDAY SPIRIT ANYTIME.

3 ½ oz sausage meat
½ small onion, peeled and diced
½ tsp garlic puree
1 tsp sage
3 Tbsp breadcrumbs
Salt and pepper, to taste

1. Place your ingredients into a mixing bowl and mix well.
2. Form into medium sized balls and place them in the air fryer.
3. Cook at 360 degrees F for 15 minutes and then serve. (Serve over pasta if desired.)

Honey Roasted Carrots

15 MINUTES » MAKES 4 SERVINGS
WITH THESE SWEET TREATS, EATING YOUR VEGGIES HAS NEVER BEEN TASTIER.

6 carrots
2 tsp honey
2 tsp chili flakes
1 tsp garlic powder (or crushed garlic)
2 tsp ghee (or coconut oil)
1 Tbsp mint (and/or coriander)
Salt, to taste

1. Peel the skin of the carrots and cut into thin long pieces.
2. Mix honey, chili flakes, garlic, salt and ghee in a bowl.
3. Toss the carrots into it and mix well, making sure the carrots are uniformly coated.
4. Preheat the air fryer at 390 degrees F for 5 minutes.
5. Transfer the prepared carrot to the basket and bake for 5 minutes.
6. Now sprinkle the mint/coriander and mix well.
7. Bake for another minute.
8. Transfer to a serving bowl and serve warm.

Tips & Tricks

Just like with a traditional cooking method, air frying will produce plenty of delicious drippings when you cook with meat, so you can save it for use in later recipes.

Starters & Sides

Brussels Sprouts

40 MINUTES » MAKES 3 SERVINGS

NO VEGETABLE HAS GONE FROM ZERO TO HERO AS DRAMATICALLY AS THE SPROUT, AND THIS AIR-FRIED VERSION IS PROOF OF WHY.

1 lb Brussels sprouts
2 tsp avocado oil
1 Tbsp seasoning of choice
Salt and pepper, to taste

1. Preheat the air fryer to 390 degrees F.
2. While the air fryer is heating up, cut the Brussels sprouts in half.
3. Remove the air fryer basket and add the Brussels sprouts, oil and seasoning.
4. Shake it all up to evenly coat everything. Place the basket back in the air fryer.
5. Set the timer for 20 to 30 minutes depending on desired crispiness.
6. Remove the basket from the air fryer every 8 to 10 minutes to shake up the Brussels sprouts so they cook evenly.
7. Once the Brussels sprouts are done cooking, remove them from the air fryer and serve!

Buttery Lemon Green Beans

20 MINUTES » MAKES 4 SERVINGS

WHETHER YOU CALL THEM GREEN BEANS OR STRING BEANS, EVERYONE CAN AGREE ON ONE THING: THE FLAVOR OF THIS CITRUSY SIDE.

1 lb green beans
2 Tbsp olive oil
2 Tbsp butter
2 cloves garlic, minced
¼ cup lemon juice
1 Tbsp Parmesan cheese

1. Start by washing the green beans, and then cutting the ends off, removing the string from the green beans.
2. Place beans in a large mixing bowl. Lightly coat with olive oil and season with salt and pepper.
3. Put the green beans in air fryer in a single layer at 390 degrees F, for 8 to 10 minutes or until done. Shake halfway through.
4. Meanwhile, make the sauce. In a small saucepan, melt the butter, then mix in the garlic and lemon juice. Heat for about 3 minutes, then mix in the Parmesan cheese and pour over the cooked green beans.
5. Plate, serve and enjoy!

Starters & Sides

Old-School Okra

35 MINUTES » MAKES 2 SERVINGS

PROVE BEYOND A DOUBT THAT YOUR TABLE HAS SOUL WITH THIS AMAZING VERSION OF A SOUTHERN CLASSIC.

7-8 oz fresh okra
1 egg
1 cup skim milk
1 cup breadcrumbs
½ tsp sea salt
Oil for misting or cooking spray

1. Remove stem ends from okra and cut in ½-inch slices.
2. In a medium bowl, beat together egg and milk. Add okra slices and stir to coat.
3. In a sealable plastic bag or container with a lid, mix together the breadcrumbs and salt.
4. Remove okra from egg mixture, letting excess drip off, and transfer into bag with breadcrumbs. Be sure okra is well-drained before placing it in the breadcrumbs. You may want to use a slotted spoon to lift a little okra at a time and let plenty of the egg wash drip off before putting it into breadcrumbs.
5. Shake okra in crumbs to coat well.
6. Place all of the coated okra into air fryer basket and mist with oil or cooking spray. Okra does not have to be in a single layer, and it isn't necessary to spray all sides at this point. A good spritz on top will do.
7. Cook at 390 degrees F for 5 minutes. Shake basket to redistribute and give it another oil spritz as you shake.
8. Cook for 5 more minutes. Shake and spray again. Cook for 2 to 5 minutes longer or until golden brown and crispy.

Plantains

25 MINUTES » MAKES 2 SERVINGS

TAKE THE AROMAS AND TASTES ON YOUR PLATE TO THE NEXT LEVEL WITH THIS SIMPLE SIDE.

2 ripe plantains (These should be almost all brown and very soft. If it were a banana, you'd say it was no good, but instead, it's a perfect plantain!)
2 tsp neutral oil (We recommend avocado oil, but sunflower or organic canola oil would also be fine.)
⅛ tsp salt (optional, but recommended)

1. Slice your plantains at an angle, cutting pieces that are about ½-inch thick.
2. Toss the plantains, oil and salt together in a medium bowl. Make sure that all of the pieces get coated in oil.
3. Transfer to your air fryer basket, and air fry at 400 degrees F for 8 to 10 minutes, shaking after 5 minutes. Your plantains are done when they're browned on the outside and tender on the inside. Cooking time will vary depending on how ripe your plantains are. Check in at 8 minutes, and add another minute or two, if needed, to reach that nice, browned outer layer.

snacks & small bites

Amuse your bouche with these air-fried plates to tide you over until the big meal.

Snacks & Small Bites

Air-Fried Pickles

35 MINUTES » MAKES 4 SERVINGS

PARDON OUR PUN, BUT THIS NEW TAKE ON A GAMEDAY FAVORITE IS DEFINITELY A VERY BIG DILL.

32 dill pickle slices
½ cup all-purpose flour
½ tsp salt
3 large eggs, lightly beaten
2 Tbsp dill pickle juice
½ tsp cayenne pepper
½ tsp garlic powder
2 cups panko
2 Tbsp snipped fresh dill
Cooking spray

1. Preheat the air fryer to 400 degrees F. Let pickles stand on a paper towel until liquid is almost absorbed, about 15 minutes.
2. Meanwhile, in a shallow bowl, combine flour and salt. In another shallow bowl, whisk eggs, pickle juice, cayenne and garlic powder. Combine panko and dill in a third shallow bowl.
3. Dip pickles in flour mixture to coat both sides; shake off excess. Dip in egg mixture, then in crumb mixture, patting to help coating adhere.
4. Spritz pickles and the air fryer basket with cooking spray.
5. Working in batches if needed, place pickles in a single layer in the air fryer basket and cook until golden brown and crispy, about 10 minutes.
6. Turn pickles; spritz with additional cooking spray. Continue cooking until golden brown and crispy, about 10 minutes.
7. Serve immediately. If desired, serve with ranch dressing.

Zucchini Chips

50 MINUTES » MAKES 3 SERVINGS

THE POTATO HAS TAKEN US FAR IN THE CHIP GAME—IT'S ZUCCHINI'S TURN AT BAT.

2 medium zucchinis,
   sliced according to your preference
¾ tsp garlic salt
1 large egg
½ cup parmesan cheese, grated
½ cup breadcrumbs
1 tsp Italian seasoning
Pepper to taste
Cooking spray

1. Prepare the zucchini for cooking, by slicing into strips or thin discs. Toss in salt and let sit for 30 minutes to remove the excess moisture. Rinse with cold water and then pat dry with paper towels.
2. Preheat air fryer to 390 degrees F.
3. Whisk the egg in a bowl and mix the cheese, breadcrumbs and Italian seasoning into another. These will serve as your breading.
4. Cover each zucchini slice with the breading by first dipping into the egg bath and then in the breadcrumbs mix.
5. Spray some cooking oil into the fry basket then place the zucchini slices inside. You can also opt to drizzle olive oil onto the slices to achieve a fried taste.
6. Cook for about 10 minutes or until crispy.
7. Serve with your dip of choice.

Snacks & Small Bites

Crispy Fried Frankfurters

12 MINUTES » MAKES 2 SERVINGS
THE RECIPE COULDN'T BE SIMPLER: NEITHER COULD THE SHEER JOY OF THIS CHILDHOOD CLASSIC.

2 hot dogs
2 hot dog buns
2 Tbsp grated cheese if desired

1. Preheat your air fryer to 390 degrees F for about 4 minutes.
2. Place two hot dogs into the air fryer, cook for about 5 minutes.
3. Remove the hot dog from air fryer.
4. Place the hot dog on a bun, add cheese if desired.
5. Place dressed hot dog into the air fryer and cook for an additional 2 minutes.

Tips & Tricks

Aerosol sprays have been known to interact poorly with the coating used in air fryer baskets, so opt for another lubrication method before you get cooking.

Your New Favorite Blueberry Muffins

15 MINUTES » MAKES 5 SERVINGS
YOU MIGHT HAVE THOUGHT THE BLUEBERRY MUFFIN WAS SIMPLY TOO GOOD TO BE IMPROVED UPON. WE ALL MAKE MISTAKES.

2 ½ cups self-rising flour
½ cup monk fruit (or your preferred sugar)
½ cup cream
¼ cup avocado oil (or any light cooking oil)
1 lemon, juiced
2 eggs
1 tsp vanilla
1 cup blueberries
Brown sugar for topping (a little sprinkling on top of each muffin—less than a teaspoon)

1. In small bowl, mix the self-rising flour and sugar together. Set aside.
2. In a medium bowl, combine cream, oil, lemon juice, eggs, vanilla and blueberries.
3. Add the flour mixture to the liquid mixture and stir just until blended.
4. Spoon the batter into silicone cupcake holders. Sprinkle ½ tsp brown sugar on top of each muffin.
5. Bake at 320 degrees F for 10 minutes, checking muffins at 6 minutes to ensure they are not cooking too fast. Put a toothpick into the center of the muffin and when the toothpick comes out clean and the muffins have browned, they are done. No need to over-bake the muffins, they will continue to cook for another minute or two after they are removed from the air fryer.
6. Remove and let cool before serving.

Snacks & Small Bites

Old Bay Chicken Wings

50 MINUTES » MAKES 6 SERVINGS

GET AN AUTHENTIC TASTE OF THE ATLANTIC COAST WITH THESE FLAVORFUL ALTERNATIVES TO BUFFALO WINGS.

3 lbs chicken wing parts
¾ cup potato starch
1 Tbsp Old Bay seasoning
½ cup butter
1 tsp True Lemon seasoning
Fresh lemon

1. Pat dry chicken wing parts.
2. Mix together potato starch and Old Bay seasoning. Add chicken wings and coat.
3. Shake off excess potato starch and place in air fryer basket.
4. Cook at 360 degrees F for 35 minutes, shaking often. Turn temperature to 400 degrees F and cook an additional 10 minutes, shaking often.
5. Melt butter with True Lemon and toss with hot wings. Serve wings with the remaining lemon butter for dipping and lemons for squeezing.

Beet Chips

30 MINUTES » MAKES 3 SERVINGS

BEAT THE BOREDOM OF PLAIN OLD CRISPS WITH THE POWER OF THE BEET.

4 small beets, about ½ lb total, peeled
2 tsp extra-virgin olive oil
Kosher salt and freshly ground pepper

1. Slice the beets very thinly, about 1/16 inch thick. Line a baking sheet with paper towels and arrange the beet slices on the towels in a single layer. Top with another layer of paper towels and press down firmly. Set aside for 10 minutes to allow the beets to dry.
2. In a large bowl, toss the beet slices with the olive oil and a generous pinch each of salt and pepper.
3. Preheat air fryer to 300 degrees F. Spray the air fryer basket with nonstick cooking spray, then arrange half of the beets in the basket in a single layer. Insert into the air fryer and cook until the beets are crisp and browned at the edges, 12 to 15 minutes. Transfer the beet chips to a platter and repeat to air fry the remaining beets. Serve immediately.

Snacks & Small Bites

Dry Rub Hot Wings

65 MINUTES » MAKES 2 SERVINGS

BRING THE HEAT WITHOUT THE NEED FOR A BOX OF WET NAPS WITH THESE CAYENNE-FUELED CLASSICS.

1 lb chicken wings, fresh or frozen, thawed
2 Tbsp paprika
2 Tbsp white sugar
1 Tbsp basil
1 Tbsp oregano
1 Tbsp garlic powder
1 Tbsp onion powder
1 Tbsp thyme
1 Tbsp white pepper
1 Tbsp black pepper
1 Tbsp cayenne pepper

1. Preheat air fryer to 400 degrees F for 4 to 5 minutes.
2. Add spices and sugar together in a bowl.
3. Stir well.
4. Dip each wing into the mix and rub both sides of the wings.
5. Place the wings in a bowl and allow to marinate for 30 to 45 minutes.
6. Arrange chicken wings in a single layer in the air fryer.
7. Air fry at 400 degrees F for 12 minutes.
8. At the halfway point, flip the wings for even cooking.

Apple Chips

20 MINUTES » MAKES 2 SERVINGS

THESE TASTY CHIPS CAN BE USED AS PART OF AN APPETIZER OR CHARCUTERIE PLATTER, OR THEY CAN BE EATEN BY THE BOWLFUL. TRUST US.

1 apple, peeled, cored and thinly sliced horizontally
½ tsp ground cinnamon
1 Tbsp sugar
Pinch of kosher salt

1. Preheat your air fryer to 390 degrees F.
2. Lay the apple slices on a baking sheet. In a small bowl, stir together the cinnamon, sugar and salt. Sprinkle the mixture evenly over the apple slices.
3. Working in batches, place the apple slices in the fry basket and insert into the air fryer. Cook until the slices are slightly golden brown, 7 to 8 minutes, turning them over halfway through cooking.
4. Transfer the chips to a bowl and let cool before serving.

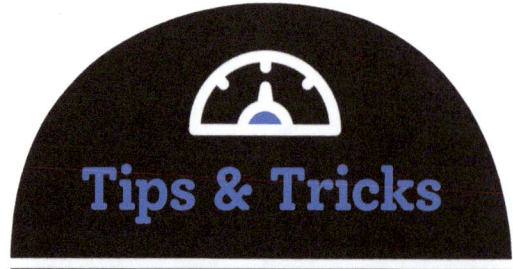

Tips & Tricks

The more you overcrowd the basket, the less surface area of your food will be exposed to the rapidly moving air, so make sure to work in small batches.

THE ULTIMATE AIR FRYER HANDBOOK

Snacks & Small Bites

Crispy Chickpeas

25 MINUTES » MAKES 3 SERVINGS

TOSS A FEW OF THESE OVER A SALAD OR TRY A FEW WITH YOUR FAVORITE SANDWICH INSTEAD OF CHIPS.

1 can chickpeas
  (drained and rinsed—no sugar added)
2 tsp olive oil
1 tsp ground cumin
1 tsp ground coriander
1 tsp garlic powder
1/8 tsp ground ginger

1. Put the rinsed beans into a medium mixing bowl and add the rest of the ingredients.
2. Stir well to coat the beans in the oil and spices.
3. Pour the beans into the food basket of your air fryer.
4. Adjust the air fryer to a temperature of 370 degrees F.
5. Cook for 12 minutes.
6. Pull out the basket and stir the beans. Put the basket back in and set again at 370 degrees F and cook for another 8 minutes.
7. Repeat the stirring process one more time, set for 370 degrees F and cook for 1 minute longer.
8. If your beans are large they may need a little longer to get a good crunch. At this point, cook and stir in 1 minute intervals until they are cooked to your liking.
9. The main idea is to stir them every few minutes throughout the process. They should have a nice little crunch to them when they have cooled.
10. Pack them in snack bags and take them with you or store them in the fridge until you are ready to eat them. Store in the fridge for up to one week. But be aware that you may have to roast them again for a minute or two to get them crunchy again if they've been in the fridge awhile. Enjoy!

Mini Spanakopita Bites

20 MINUTES » MAKES 3 SERVINGS

WHIP UP A BATCH OF THESE GREEK FLAVOR BOMBS ON A SUNDAY FOR ALL-WEEK SNACKING, OR PULL OUT ALL THE STOPS FOR THE NEXT BIG GAME.

1 (10-oz) bag frozen chopped spinach
1 (4-oz) package feta cheese
2 eggs, beaten
Salt and pepper to taste
2 (1.9-oz) mini phyllo shells

1. Thaw your frozen spinach. Then drain as much liquid out of the spinach as you can.
2. Mix the drained spinach with feta, egg, salt and pepper.
3. Spoon the combined mixture into the phyllo shells. (To prevent them from flying around, put the filled pies into a muffin tin.)
4. Set the temperature to 220 degrees F and the time for 4 minutes. Check to make sure they are hot and bubbling. If not, add another 3 minutes.
5. Remove from the air fryer, plate, serve and enjoy!

Snacks & Small Bites

Prawn Crackers

20 MINUTES » MAKES 5 SERVINGS

ADD DEPTH TO THIS FAVORITE FROM ACROSS THE POND BY WORKING WITH YOUR AIR FRYER.

3 cups dried prawn crackers
1 Tbsp oil

1. Preheat the air fryer to 390 degrees F.
2. In a large mixing bowl, add oil to dried prawn crackers.
3. Toss and ensure that each piece of the prawn crackers is coated thoroughly with the oil.
4. Divide the crackers and air fry in batches (about 3 pieces each batch).
5. Air fry for about 2 to 3 mins at 390 degrees F or until golden brown. Pull out the basket and shake halfway during frying (or use a tong to "stir").
6. Continue with the remaining batches until all the crackers are fried.
7. Cool and store in airtight container.

Banana Chips

30 MINUTES » MAKES 4 SERVINGS

BE HONEST: THESE LITTLE BEAUTIES ARE JUST ABOUT THE ONLY REASON YOU BUY TRAIL MIX. CUT OUT THE MIDDLEMAN WITH YOUR AIR FRYER.

3-4 ripe bananas
½ tsp turmeric powder
1 tsp salt, plus more for seasoning
1 tsp of your preferred cooking oil
½ tsp chaat masala
Honey, as desired

1. Peel the bananas and keep aside.
2. Prepare a mixture of water, turmeric powder and salt. Cut slices of banana in this mixture. It will prevent the bananas from turning black and also give a nice yellow color.
3. Keep bananas soaked in this mixture for 5 to 10 minutes.
4. Drain the water and dry the chips.
5. Apply a little oil on chips to prevent them sticking together in the air fryer.
6. Preheat the air fryer at 350 degrees F for 5 minutes.
7. Air fry the chips for about 15 minutes at 350 degrees F.
8. Add salt, chaat masala and honey.

Tips & Tricks

When air frying bite sized items like banana chips or french fries, be sure to shake the basket occasionally during cooking to make sure that all sides of the pieces are exposed to the hot air directly.

THE ULTIMATE AIR FRYER HANDBOOK

Snacks & Small Bites

Air-Fry Eggplant Fritters

70 MINUTES » MAKES 3 SERVINGS

PAIR THESE PERFECT MORSELS WITH TOMATO SAUCE OR YOUR FAVORITE DIP FOR A SATISFYING NOSH.

1 medium (1-1 ¼ lbs.) eggplant, sliced into strips
¾ tsp garlic salt
2 large eggs
½ cup wheat germ, toasted
½ cup parmesan cheese, grated
1 tsp Italian seasoning
2 Tbsp olive oil or cooking spray

1. Slice the eggplant up according to your desired fry size and length, then add some garlic salt for seasoning. Let sit for up to 45 minutes to remove excess moisture.
2. Preheat your air fryer to 400 degrees F.
3. In one bowl, whisk the eggs. In another, mix the wheat germ, cheese and seasonings. These will serve as your breading.
4. Dip the sliced eggplants into the egg and then cover it with the breading.
5. Spray the cooking basket with some cooking oil. Place the eggplant slices inside the fry basket and cook for 5 to 7 minutes before turning the ingredients. Make sure not to overcrowd your fry basket when cooking this dish as it needs better air penetration due to the breading.
6. Turn and cook for another 5 to 7 minutes or until the eggplant fritters are crispy.

Pita Pizza

10 MINUTES » MAKES 1 SERVING

THE PERFECT AFTER-SCHOOL SNACK IS ALSO THE PERFECT BITE FOR A PECKISH GROWN-UP.

1 pita bread
1 Tbsp marinara sauce
¼ cup mozzarella cheese
1 drizzle extra virgin olive oil

1. Use a spoon and swirl marinara sauce onto pita bread.
2. Add your cheese on top.
3. Add a little drizzle of extra virgin olive oil over top of pizza.
4. Place in air fryer pizza pan and then place in air fryer basket.
5. Cook at 350 degrees F for 6 minutes.
6. Carefully remove from air fryer and cut.

Tasty, low-carb recipes to jump-start the new you!

AVAILABLE AT ONNEWSSTANDSNOW.COM

main courses

Here they are: the stars of your shiny new air fryer spectacular.

All-American Burgers
Recipe on page 52

Main Courses

Country-Style Air-Fried Steak

30 MINUTES » MAKES 4 SERVINGS
YOU AND YOURS WILL LOVE ALL THE DOWN-HOME COMFORT WITH ALMOST NONE OF THE GUILT.

2 lbs rib eye steak
1 Tbsp steak rub
1 Tbsp olive oil

1. To preheat the air fryer, scroll to the French Fries setting.
2. Adjust the cooking time to 4 minutes at 400 degrees F to preheat.
3. Season the steak on both sides with rub and olive oil.
4. Place steak in the fry basket.
5. Scroll to the Steak setting.
6. Adjust cooking time to 14 minutes at 400 degrees F.
7. After 7 minutes, flip the steak.
8. When the timer is done, remove steak from the air fryer. Let rest for 10 minutes before slicing and serving.

Main Courses

All-American Burgers

20 MINUTES » MAKES 4 SERVINGS

WHEN IT'S TOO COLD OUTSIDE TO FIRE UP THE GRILL, LOOK NO FURTHER THAN THESE AIR-FRIED TREATS.

1 Tbsp Worcestershire sauce
1 tsp Maggi seasoning sauce
Liquid smoke (few drops)
½ tsp garlic powder
½ tsp onion powder
½ tsp salt (or salt sub)
½ tsp ground black pepper
1 tsp parsley (dried)
1 lb ground beef

1. Set air fryer temperature to 350 degrees F.
2. In a small bowl, mix together all the seasoning items, from the Worcestershire sauce down to and including the dried parsley.
3. Add this to the beef in a large bowl.
4. Mix well but be careful not to overwork the meat as that leads to tough burgers.
5. Divide the beef mixture into 4 and shape the patties. With your thumb, put an indent in the center of each one to prevent the patties from bunching up in the middle.
6. Put patties in the air fryer and spray tops of patties lightly with oil.
7. Cook 10 minutes for medium (or longer to desired degree of doneness). There is no need to turn the patties.
8. Serve hot on a bun with toppings of your choice.

The Holiday Turkey of the Future

75 MINUTES » MAKES 16 SERVINGS

REMEMBER THAT TIME YOUR CRAZY UNCLE ALMOST BURNED THE HOUSE DOWN WITH HIS D.I.Y. DEEP FRYER? NEVER AGAIN.

8 lbs turkey breast, bone in
2 Tbsp sea salt
1 Tbsp black pepper
2 Tbsp olive oil

1. Season the turkey and rub with olive oil.
2. Place the turkey breast side down in the fry basket.
3. Scroll to the Chicken setting.
4. Adjust cooking time to 20 minutes at 360 degrees F.
5. When the timer is done, carefully turn the breast over.
6. Scroll to the Chicken setting.
7. Adjust cooking time to 20 minutes at 360 degrees F.
8. Test the turkey with a thermometer for proper doneness (165 degrees F).
9. Let turkey rest 20 minutes before serving.

Main Courses

Not Your Nonna's Italian Meatballs

40 MINUTES » MAKES 5 SERVINGS

THEY'D NEVER HEARD OF AN AIR FRYER WHEN SHE LEARNED TO MAKE THEM, BUT THAT DOESN'T MEAN YOU HAVE TO CHOOSE AN INFERIOR METHOD.

2 lbs ground beef (choose your preferred cuts)
2 large eggs
1 ¼ cups breadcrumbs
   (or 3 slices of slightly stale bread made into crumbs with grater or food processor)
¼ cup chopped fresh parsley
1 tsp dried oregano (optional)
¼ cup grated Parmigiano-Reggiano
1 small clove garlic, chopped
Salt and pepper, to taste
1 tsp light oil dabbed on a paper towel
   to coat the air fryer basket

1. Place the meat and all the ingredients in a large mixing bowl.
2. Mix all the ingredients together with your hands. You can use a wooden spoon to begin the mixing process but using your hands is the best way to blend everything together. Mix the ingredients just until everything is well blended.
3. Scoop up a small handful of meat and roll in the palm of your hand to your desired size meatball (approximately 2-inch round). Or you can use a cookie scoop which will give you even-sized meatballs.
4. Lightly coat the air fryer basket with light oil, spread on with a paper towel.
5. Cook meatballs at 350 degrees F for 10 to 13 minutes until lightly browned. Turn them over and cook another 4 to 5 minutes. Remove to a plate when baked.
6. When ready, place meatballs into the tomato sauce to continue cooking until sauce is done.
7. Serve on a hero roll or with your favorite pasta.

Main Courses

Beef Empanadas

20-30 MINUTES » MAKES 8 SERVINGS
SWITCH UP YOUR RED MEAT DELIVERY METHOD BY OPTING FOR THESE WONDERFUL POCKETS OF FLAVOR.

8 Goya empanada discs (in frozen section), thawed
1 cup picadillo
1 egg white, whisked
1 tsp water

1. Preheat the air fryer to 325 degrees F for 8 minutes. Spray the basket generously with cooking spray.
2. Place 2 Tbsp picadillo in the center of each disc. Fold in half and use a fork to seal the edges. Repeat with the remaining dough.
3. Whisk the egg whites with water, then brush the tops of the empanadas.
4. Bake 2 or 3 at a time in the air fryer for 8 minutes, or until golden. Remove from heat and repeat with the remaining empanadas.

BBQ Ribs

20-30 MINUTES » MAKES 6 SERVINGS
ENJOY ALL THE FLAVOR WITH LESS MESS AND MORE TIME WITH THE FAMILY.

2-3 lbs baby back ribs
32 oz BBQ sauce (your favorite)
Salt & pepper to taste

1. Start by preheating your air fryer to 390 degrees F. (You don't have to preheat, but it might give the ribs more flavor.)
2. Season the ribs with salt and pepper and other spices if you like. Remove the membrane.
3. Smother your ribs with BBQ sauce and place them in your air fryer basket.
4. Set the time for 10 minutes, then flip them again for 7 minutes.
5. Remove from the air fryer, add some extra sauce if you wish, plate, serve & enjoy!

NOTE: *You should always use a thermometer for pork, as eating raw pork can cause illness.*

Tips & Tricks

Just like regular ovens, air fryers can run a little hot or cold depending on the model and the conditions you're cooking in. So get to know your machine as best you can.

Main Courses

Cheesy Chicken Quesadillas

15-20 MINUTES » MAKES 2 SERVINGS

TURN TACO TUESDAY ON ITS HEAD WITH THESE AIR-FRIED 'DILLAS.

4 soft taco shells
⅓ cup shredded Mexican cheese
1 package frozen chicken fajita strips
½ cup sliced green peppers
½ cup sliced onions
Salsa (optional)
Sour cream (optional)

1. Preheat air fryer on 370 degrees F for about 3 minutes.
2. Spray cooking basket lightly with vegetable oil.
3. Place 1 soft taco shell in the basket.
4. Place shredded cheese on shell. You can use as much or as little as you'd like.
5. Lay out fajita chicken strips so they are in a single layer.
6. Put your onions and green peppers on top of your chicken.
7. Add more shredded cheese.
8. Place another soft taco shell on top and spray lightly with vegetable oil. You can use the rack that came with the air fryer on top of the shell to hold it in place.
9. Set timer for 4 minutes.
10. Flip over carefully with a large spatula.
11. Spray lightly with vegetable oil and place rack on top of shell to hold it in place.
12. Set timer for 4 minutes.
13. If it's not crispy enough for you, leave in for a couple of extra minutes.
14. Remove and cut into 4 slices or 6 slices.
15. Serve with salsa and sour cream if desired.

Tofu Delight

30 MINUTES » MAKES 3 SERVINGS

TAKE YOUR HEALTH FOOD TREND TO THE FAR EAST AND TEACH YOUR FAMILY THE DELIGHTS OF SOYBEANS.

1 block tofu, chopped into 1-inch pieces
2 Tbsp soy sauce
2 Tbsp olive oil, divided
1 tsp turmeric
½ tsp garlic powder
½ tsp onion powder
½ cup chopped onion
2 ½ cups chopped red potato, 1-inch cubes, (about 2-3 potatoes)
4 cups broccoli florets

1. In a medium-sized bowl, toss together the tofu, soy sauce, 1 Tbsp olive oil, turmeric, garlic powder, onion powder and onion. Set aside to marinate.
2. In a separate, small bowl, toss the potatoes in the remaining olive oil, and air fry at 400 degrees F for 15 minutes, shaking once around 7 to 8 minutes into cooking.
3. Shake the potatoes again, then add the tofu, reserving any leftover marinade. Set the tofu and potatoes to cook at 370 degrees F for 15 more minutes and start the air fryer.
4. While the tofu is cooking, toss the broccoli in the reserved marinade. If there isn't enough to get it all over the broccoli, add a little bit of extra soy sauce. Dry broccoli is not your friend. When there are 5 minutes of cooking time remaining, add the broccoli to the air fryer.
5. Serve in hot tomato sauce if desired.

Main Courses

Chicken Tikka

20-30 MINUTES » MAKES 3 SERVINGS

THERE'S A REASON THIS DISH IS THE BEST-SELLER AT YOUR LOCAL INDIAN RESTAURANT. NOW YOU CAN RECREATE IT AT HOME.

1 lb chicken thighs, cut into bite-size cubes
½ cup Greek yogurt
1 tsp curry powder
1 tsp Garam Masala
½ tsp smoked paprika
¼ tsp cayenne pepper (optional)
1 Tbsp olive oil
1 tsp salt
Oil spray or mist
1 large green pepper,
  cut into large chunks (optional)
1 large red onion, chopped (optional)
Lemons and cilantro to garnish

1. In a large bowl or a resealable bag, combine the cubed chicken, yogurt, curry powder, Garam Masala, smoked paprika, cayenne pepper (if using), olive oil and salt. Give it a good mix and marinate, in the fridge, anywhere between 2 hours to overnight.
2. If using wooden skewers, soak them in water for 2 hours.
3. Skewer each chicken piece, alternating with green pepper chunks and red onion chunks, onto metal or soaked wooden skewers.
4. Lightly grease the air fryer basket.
5. Add the skewers to the basket and air fry at 360 degrees F for 15 minutes.
6. Serve the Chicken Tikka with a squeeze of lemon juice and a sprinkling of chopped cilantro.
NOTE: It pairs great with Indian basmati rice or any kind of Indian bread like naan or even pita bread.

Reuben Calzones

30 MINUTES » MAKES 2 SERVINGS

CAN'T DECIDE ON WHICH NEW YORK STAPLE YOU'RE CRAVING? EMBRACE THE MELTING POT AND COMBINE THE TWO.

1 (13.8-oz) tube refrigerated pizza crust
4 slices Swiss cheese
1 cup sauerkraut, rinsed and well drained
½ lb sliced cooked corned beef
Thousand Island salad dressing

1. Preheat air fryer to 400 degrees F. Spritz air fryer basket with cooking spray.
2. On a lightly floured surface, unroll pizza crust dough and pat into a 12-inch square. Cut into four squares. Layer one slice of the cheese and a fourth of the sauerkraut and corned beef diagonally over half of each square to within ½-inch of edges. Fold one corner over filling to the opposite corner, forming a triangle; press edges with a fork to seal. Place two calzones in a single layer in greased air fryer basket.
3. Cook until calzones are golden brown, 8 to 12 minutes, flipping halfway through cooking. Remove and keep warm; repeat with remaining calzones. Serve with salad dressing.

Main Courses

Marinated Steak

15 MINUTES » MAKES 2 SERVINGS
KICK THE FLAVOR UP ON YOUR EVERYDAY CUTS WITH THIS FLAVORFUL RECIPE.

2 New York strip steaks, any cut
1 Tbsp low-sodium soy sauce
1 tsp liquid smoke
1 Tbsp McCormick's Grill Mates Montreal Steak seasoning or steak rub (or season to taste)
½ Tbsp unsweetened cocoa powder
Salt and pepper, to taste
Melted butter (optional)

1. Drizzle the steaks with the soy sauce and liquid smoke. You can do this inside zip top bags.
2. Season the steak with the seasonings.
3. Refrigerate for at least a couple of hours, preferably overnight.
4. Place the steak in the air fryer. Do not use any oil. Cook two steaks at a time (if air fryer is standard size). You can use an accessory grill pan, a layer rack or the standard air fryer basket.
5. Cook for 5 minutes at 375 degrees F. After 5 minutes, open the air fryer and examine your steak. Cook time will vary depending on your desired doneness. Check the inside of the steaks to determine if they have finished cooking. You can stick a knife or fork in the center to review the level of pink. You can also use a meat thermometer and cook to 125 degrees F for rare, 135 degrees F for medium-rare, 145 degrees F for medium, 155 degrees F for medium-well and 160 degrees F for well done.
6. For medium steak, at 5 minutes, flip the steak and cook for an additional 2 minutes, 7 minutes cook time total using the air fryer.
7. Remove the steak from the air fryer and drizzle with melted butter.

Main Courses

Salmon Patties

15 MINUTES » MAKES 2 SERVINGS

FRESH SALMON ISN'T JUST DELICIOUS, IT'S GREAT FOR YOU. SO DIG IN AND FEEL GOOD ABOUT IT.

14 ¾ oz salmon
1 egg
¼ cup diced onion
1 tsp dill weed
½ cup breadcrumbs

1. Start by cleaning the fish, remove the bones and skin.
2. Mix the egg, onion, dill weed and breadcrumbs into the salmon.
3. Mix well.
4. Shape into patties. Place them in the air fryer.
5. Set the temperature for 370 degrees F. Cook for 5 minutes, then flip them and air fry for another 5 minutes.
6. Plate, serve and enjoy!

Tips & Tricks

The air fryer is at its best when making tasty meals for one or two people. While it can handle more in batches, making air fryer food for the whole clan can be time consuming, so plan accordingly.

Cornish Game Hen

50 MINUTES » MAKES 4 SERVINGS

A CLASSIC GAME BIRD WITH SOME CLASSIC SEASONING—A RECIPE FOR SUCCESS.

1-2 ½ lbs Cornish hen
1 cup buttermilk
1 cup seasoned flour
2 eggs, slightly beaten
1 cup panko breadcrumbs
Coconut oil spray

1. Rinse and place Cornish hen in a zip top bag with enough buttermilk to cover. Place bag in a bowl to prevent leakage. Refrigerate for 2 to 24 hours.
2. Set up a dipping station with seasoned flour, egg and panko crumbs.
3. Remove hen from buttermilk, allowing the excess buttermilk to drip off. Discard buttermilk. Dredge hen in the seasoned flour making sure to cover the entire hen. Then dip hen into the beaten eggs, and finally coat with the panko crumbs.
4. Spray lightly with coconut oil spray for extra crispy skin.
5. Place hen in air-fryer and "cook" for 30 minutes at 360 degrees F or until internal temperature is 165 degrees F.
6. Allow to rest for about 5 minutes and serve with your favorite side dish.

Main Courses

Crispy Pollock

20 MINUTES » MAKES 2 SERVINGS

SERVE THIS ALONGSIDE CHIPS FOR A FANCY THROWBACK TO THE BRITISH ISLES.

2 pollock filets
Salt and pepper, to taste
1 egg, whisked
½ cup breadcrumbs, plus more if needed

1. Season the fish with salt and pepper.
2. Let dry for 10 minutes before dredging through the egg.
3. Dredge through the egg and then cover with the breadcrumbs and place in your spray-oiled air fryer.
4. Cook at 370 degrees F for 8 minutes.
5. Enjoy!

Tips & Tricks

To ensure that your air fryer operates at its best, allow at least five inches on all sides for air flow. And never, ever put anything on top of your air fryer.

THE ULTIMATE AIR FRYER HANDBOOK

Main Courses

Cauliflower Pizza

30 MINUTES » MAKES 2 SERVINGS
WE ALL LOVE PIZZA, BUT MORE AND MORE OF US DON'T LIKE CARBS. PROBLEM SOLVED WITH THIS CAULI CRUST CLASSIC.

½ package organic riced cauliflower, steamed
2 whole eggs
1 cup mozzarella
1 Tbsp Flavor God Garlic Lovers seasoning, or whatever seasoning you like
¼ cup psyllium powder
Pizza toppings, whatever you prefer

1. Steam your riced cauliflower in the microwave until it is tender, about 3 to 4 minutes.
2. Put cauliflower in a strainer and push out as much water as you can using the back of a spoon.
3. Preheat your air fryer for 5 minutes at 400 degrees F.
4. Put all of the ingredients into a bowl except the psyllium. Mix together.
5. Start adding the psyllium as you are mixing. When the mix starts to look dry you are done.
6. Put "dough" into air fryer being careful not to burn yourself. Flatten it out to your desired thickness and so it's not quite touching the edges.
7. Cook in air fryer at 400 degrees F for 10 to 15 minutes until it is golden brown.
8. Put your preferred toppings on the pizza crust and put back in the air fryer to melt the cheese.

Main Courses

Zoodles and Meatballs

30 MINUTES » MAKES 3 SERVINGS

WHO NEEDS CARBS? NOT YOU, NOW THAT YOU HAVE THIS ZOODLE-BASED RECIPE.

1 lb ground beef
3 Tbsp flaxseed meal (optional)
1 dash liquid smoke (optional)
1 dash McCormick Montreal Steak Seasoning or whatever you prefer
1 cup spaghetti sauce
2 medium zucchini, spiralized

1. Mix hamburger, flaxseed meal, liquid smoke and seasoning. Form into meatballs and place in the air fryer basket.
2. Set the air fryer to meat presetting and let your fryer do its magic! You'll want to check on your meatballs a little over the halfway point to roll them around a bit for even cooking.
3. Put the spaghetti sauce in a small saucepan and warm or reduce as you like it, over low heat.
4. Zoodle up your zucchini. If you don't have a tabletop or handheld spiralizer, you can use a julienne peeler or even mandoline.
5. With about 5 minutes left on your meatballs and after you've rolled them about the fryer basket, pile your zoodles on top.
6. Cook a couple of minutes, and then pop open the air fryer and flip the zoodles. When the zoodles are warm, "al dente" texture and maybe have a hint of browning, consider them done.
7. Serve it up. Heats up great for leftovers (if you have any left, that is).

Pub Standard Mince Pies

25 MINUTES » MAKES 2 SERVINGS

IT DOESN'T GET MORE OLD SCHOOL THAN THIS BIT OF ENGLISH PUB FOOD. GIVE YOUR GUESTS A HISTORY LESSON WITH THEIR DELICIOUS DISH.

½ lb plain flour
¼ lb butter
1 oz caster sugar
¼ lb mincemeat
1 medium egg, beaten

1. Preheat the air fryer to 350 degrees F
2. Start by making your sweet pastry. In a mixing bowl, mix your butter into your flour until it resembles fine breadcrumbs. Add the sugar and mix well. Add a little warm water at a time while mixing at the same time until your mixture makes lovely soft dough.
3. Roll out your pastry using a little extra flour to stop it sticking. Place pastry into each of the pastry cases that you're using. Then fill each one with mincemeat.
4. Add another layer of pastry on top and then slit with a knife so the mince pies have room to breathe. Brush the top with egg.
5. Place in the air fryer for 12 minutes at 350 degrees F.

Main Courses

Shrimp Parm

20 MINUTES » MAKES 3 SERVINGS

YOU'LL HAVE A HARD TIME GOING BACK TO REGULAR OLD CHICKEN CUTLETS AGAIN AFTER YOU EAT THIS SEAFOOD VERSION.

2 lbs jumbo cooked shrimp, peeled and deveined
4 cloves garlic, minced
2/3 cup parmesan cheese, grated
1 tsp pepper
½ tsp oregano
1 tsp basil
1 tsp onion powder
2 Tbsp olive oil
Lemon, quartered

1. In a large bowl, combine garlic, parmesan cheese, pepper, oregano, basil, onion powder and olive oil.
2. Gently toss shrimp in mixture until evenly coated.
3. Spray air fryer basket with non-stick spray and place shrimp in basket.
4. Cook at 350 degrees F for 8 to 10 minutes or until seasoning on shrimp is browned.
5. Squeeze the lemon over the shrimp before serving.

Tuna Cutlets

15 MINUTES » MAKES 2 SERVINGS

SURE, YOU COULD GO FOR A TUNA-MAYO SALAD ON WHITE BREAD. BUT WHY WOULD YOU WHEN YOU'RE JUST A FEW MINUTES AWAY FROM THIS AMAZING DISH.

1 onion, chopped
1 green chile, seeded and chopped
1 Tbsp grated ginger
1 can of albacore tuna, strained
1 medium sized potato, boiled
2 Tbsp celery
1 cup breadcrumbs
1 egg
Oil for brushing
Salt to taste

1. Heat ½ Tbsp oil in a frying pan and saute chopped onions, green chile and ginger for a few minutes. As soon as the onions turn translucent, add the drained tuna to the pan and fry till all the liquid gets absorbed.
2. Remove the tuna to a plate and let it cool down. Add mashed potato and chopped celery, adjust salt and mix well to make the cutlet patty dough.
3. Make balls of the dough and shape them.
4. Beat the egg in a bowl and spread the breadcrumbs on a plate. Roll each cutlet in breadcrumbs, dip in egg and roll in crumbs again.
5. Arrange the cutlets in a preheated air fryer tray, brush lightly with oil and run the air fryer for about 2-3 minutes. Apply oil again with a brush on the cutlets and allow them to get crispy golden. This will take about 4 to 5 more minutes.
6. Serve the cutlets hot on top of crackers if desired.

Yedi®
HOUSEWARE

AIR FRYERS | PRESSURE COOKERS | AIR FRYER OVENS | SOUS VIDES
COFFEE MAKERS | PANINI MAKERS | AIR FRYER LIDS AND MORE!

Voted "BEST AIR FRYER" in 2018, 2019, 2020

"The YEDI HOUSEWARE DELUXE DIGITAL AIR FRYER is our *top pick* thanks to its large capacity and built-in smart programs that make perfect cooking incredibly easy."
- BUSINESS INSIDER

"The YEDI TOTAL PACKAGE PRESSURE COOKER, selected to the *2019 Oprah's Favorite Things List.*"

Shop Online
YEDIHOUSEWAREAPPLIANCES.COM

TOP 8
Yedi Houseware Air Fryer Tips

1. **Preheat your Yedi Air Fryer before adding your food**
   - Just like an oven, your Yedi air fryer benefits from a few minutes of preheating. To do so, just turn it on before adding your food to the cooking basket. It's a simple step that many people.

2. **Use the right kind of oils**
   - If you want to use olive oil in your Yedi Air Fryer, avoid extra-virgin varieties, which have smoke points between 350° and 410°F, and go with regular varieties which have smoke points between 390° and 470°F.
   - Oils with high smoking points, such as safflower or soybean oil are ideal for using in air fryers, as the temperatures within the machine can get very hot.

3. **Do not use non-stick aerosol cooking sprays, can cause damage to your Yedi Air Fryer.**
   - Many non-stick cooking sprays contain additives that can damage the nonstick coatings on some air fryer baskets, so you'll want to avoid using them. As an alternative, you can purchase a standard spray bottle and fill it up with your own oil.

4. **Shake the basket a few times during cooking**
   - To make sure your food is cooking evenly, *give the basket a few shakes during cooking*. You can keep the Yedi air fryer running and just remove the basket without any problems. This is especially useful for small items that you want to crisp all over, like fries or small roasted veggies.

5. **Make sure you don't overcrowd your Yedi Air Fryer basket**
   - If you add too many items to your Yedi air fryer basket, the air won't be able to circulate properly and your food won't get crispy. If you're making a large amount of something, cook items in batches instead of all at once.

6. **Cook larger size foods in a single layer & don't stack them**
   - Steaks, pork chops, fish fillets, and burgers need to be cooked in a single layer in the air fryer. If you try to stack them, the sides that are touching will end up colorless and soggy. If you can only fit three steaks at a time in the bottom of your air fryer basket and want to cook more, you'll need to cook them in batches.

7. **Use parchment paper to make cleanup easier.**
   - The Yedi Air Fryer comes with a set of 50 perforated papers that make keeping your air fryer easy. Place the perforated papers in cooking basket before placing your food in the basket.
   - Parchment paper and foil are both safe to use.

8. **Clean your Yedi Air Fryer after every use**
   - Clean the Yedi Air Fryer and accessories after every use.
   - Do not put in Dishwasher.
   - Do not use metal kitchen utensils or abrasive cleaning materials to clean any parts or pieces, as this may damage the non-stick coating.
   - Wipe the outside of the Air Fryer & accessories with a moist cloth or non-abrasive sponge.
   - If dirt is stuck to the cooking basket or the bottom of the outer basket, fill the outer basket with hot water and with some washing liquid/soap. Put the Inner Fry basket in the Outside Basket and let the baskets soak for 10 mins before wiping dry.

yedihousewareappliances.com | @yedihouseware | info@yedihouseware.com

SPECIAL BONUS SECTION

comfort classics

One of the many benefits of the air fryer is that you can indulge in favorites with less guilt. So dig into these old standards and leave room for dessert!

Classic Mac & Cheese
Recipe on page 86

Comfort Classics

Pizzeria-Style Hot Wings

35 MINUTES » MAKES 3 SERVINGS

WHETHER IT'S GAME DAY, COOKOUT NIGHT OR JUST TO SATISFY A CRAVING, THESE HOT WINGS HAVE THE FLAVOR SEALED IN WITH AIR FRYING.

12 raw chicken wings (drumettes and flats, according to your preference)
1 cup buffalo sauce

1. Place the wings into the fry basket.
2. Scroll to the French Fries setting.
3. Adjust cooking time to 25 minutes at 400 degrees F.
4. Halfway through cooking, flip the wings.
5. When done, remove and toss with buffalo sauce.
6. Return the wings to the air fryer. Scroll to the French Fries setting and cook for 8 more minutes at 400 degrees F.

Tips & Tricks

When it comes to reheating, ditch your microwave. Leftovers from the air fryer taste much better (and are much less soggy).

THE ULTIMATE AIR FRYER HANDBOOK

Comfort Classics

Fried Oysters

45 MINUTES » MAKES 2 SERVINGS

FOR A PO' BOY TOPPING OR A PERFECT FINGER FOOD FOR YOUR NEXT COOKOUT, AIR FRY SOME SHUCKED GOODNESS.

2 large eggs
3 Tbsp hot sauce
½ cup all-purpose flour
½ tsp Creole or Cajun seasoning
1 cup panko or breadcrumbs
12 plump fresh oysters, shucked
Salt and pepper to taste
Cooking oil spray

1. In one bowl, whisk the eggs and hot sauce together. Put the flour and seasoning in another. Crush the panko or breadcrumbs a bit finer and then place them in a third shallow bowl.
2. Grab a baking sheet and line it with parchment paper.
3. Cover the oysters first in flour, then shake off the excess before dipping each piece in the egg mixture. Again, shake the excess before rolling them around in the breadcrumbs.
4. Place all of the oysters in the baking sheet. Once they're all lined up, refrigerate for 30 minutes.
5. Spray oil lightly on the fry basket before placing the refrigerated oysters inside.
6. Set the air fryer to 400 degrees F for 2 minutes then start cooking. Shake the fry basket occasionally, checking the doneness of the oysters as you do.
7. Once done, remove from the fry basket and sprinkle with salt.
8. Serve on a po'boy or over greens.

County Fair Corn Dog Nuggets

25 MINUTES » MAKES 2 SERVINGS

YOU DON'T HAVE TO WAIT FOR YOUR FAVORITE STAND NEXT TO THE TILT-A-WHIRL TO OPEN UP—MAKE YOUR FAVORITE CARNIVAL SNACK AT HOME WITH LESS GREASY GUILT!

2 hot dogs, uncured
2 large eggs
1 ½ cups crushed cornflakes
½ cup all-purpose flour
8 tsp yellow mustard
Cooking spray
12 bamboo skewers or craft sticks

1. Slice each hot dog into halves then cut them up into three portions. Insert a bamboo skewer or wooden stick into each piece.
2. Crack the eggs and whisk in a shallow bowl, then place the crushed cornflakes in another. Put the flour in a third separate shallow bowl.
3. Dip each hot dog into the flour first then the egg and last into the cornflakes bowl. Try to press the cornflakes into the hot dog a bit so the small bits will stick.
4. Lightly spritz some cooking oil into the fry basket then place the corn dogs inside.
5. Set the air fryer to 375 degrees F and cook for 5 minutes. Turn the corn dogs and then resume cooking for 5 more minutes or until the breading becomes crispy.
6. Serve with mustard.

Comfort Classics

Western Frittata

15 MINUTES » MAKES 1 SERVING

YOU'LL FEEL LIKE YOU'RE AT YOUR FAVORITE GREASY SPOON—WITHOUT THE GREASE—WHEN YOU DIG INTO THIS HEARTY BREAKFAST.

1 breakfast sausage patty
2 large eggs
1 Tbsp chopped spring onions
1 Tbsp chopped bell peppers
2 Tbsp cheddar cheese
1 Tbsp melted butter

1. Generously grease a 4-inch cake pan or a mini loaf pan (or any oven safe pan that fits in your air-fryer basket) with butter.
2. Add the chopped-up breakfast sausage in the greased pan and air fry at 350 degrees F for 5 minutes.
3. Meanwhile, in a medium sized bowl, crack the eggs. Add salt and pepper and whisk well.
4. Add the chopped spring onion and bell peppers and mix well. Once the sausage is cooked, add the egg mixture. Mix well with the sausages.
5. Sprinkle with cheddar cheese and air fry at 350 F for another 5 minutes.
6. Serve hot with fresh tomato salsa for a delicious low-carb breakfast.

Scotch Eggs

25 MINUTES » MAKES 4 SERVINGS

THIS BRITISH FAVORITE HAS GAINED NEW POPULARITY ACROSS THE POND THANKS TO ITS LOW CARB PROFILE AND ON-THE-GO POSSIBILITIES.

1 lb bulk pork sausage
2 tsp coarse-ground mustard, plus more for serving
1 Tbsp finely chopped fresh chives
2 Tbsp finely chopped fresh parsley
⅛ tsp freshly grated nutmeg
⅛ tsp salt
⅛ tsp ground black pepper
4 hard-cooked eggs, peeled
1 cup shredded parmesan cheese

1. In a large bowl combine sausage, mustard, chives, parsley, nutmeg, salt and black pepper. Gently mix until everything is well combined. Shape mixture into four equal-size patties.
2. Please each egg on a sausage patty and shape sausage around egg. Dip each in shredded Parmesan cheese to cover completely, pressing lightly to adhere. Make sure the cheese shreds are well-pressed into the meat, so that they do not fly around in the air fryer.
3. Arrange eggs in air fryer basket. Spray lightly with nonstick vegetable oil. Set fryer to 400 degrees F for 15 minutes. Halfway through cook time, turn eggs and spray with vegetable oil.
4. Serve with coarse-ground mustard.

82 THE ULTIMATE AIR FRYER HANDBOOK

Comfort Classics

Mozzarella Sticks

1 HOUR 20 MINUTES » MAKES 3 SERVINGS

AUTHENTIC ITALIAN CUISINE? NOT EXACTLY. ABSOLUTELY DELICIOUS AND A PARTY PLATTER MUST-HAVE? YOU BET YOUR BUFALA.

1 lb mozzarella cheese
1 cup breadcrumbs
¼ cup white flour
3 Tbsp nonfat milk
2 eggs

1. Cut cheese into 3 x ½-inch sticks.
2. Place breadcrumbs, flour and the combined milk and eggs each in separate bowls.
3. Dip cheese sticks in the flour, then the egg-milk mixture and finally the breadcrumbs.
4. Lay breaded sticks on a flat cookie sheet.
5. Freeze for 1 to 2 hours or until solid.
6. Place small batches of breaded sticks (do not overcrowd) into the fry basket.
7. Scroll to the French Fries setting.
8. Cook for 12 minutes at 400 degrees F.

Old Fashioned Fish Sticks

30 MINUTES » MAKES 3 SERVINGS

THERE WAS ONLY ONE WAY TO MAKE THIS COMFORT FOOD EVEN MORE AMAZING: AIR FRY IT.

2 cups panko breadcrumbs
1 cup white flour
3 Tbsp milk
2 large eggs
1 lb cod
½ tsp black pepper
¼ tsp sea salt
Tartar sauce for dipping

1. Place breadcrumbs, flour and the combined milk and eggs each in separate bowls.
2. Cut fish into 3 x ½-inch sticks.
3. Season the fish with salt and pepper. Dip the fish sticks into the flour, then the egg mixture and finally the breadcrumbs.
4. Place fish sticks into the fry basket.
5. Scroll to the Fish setting.
6. Cook for 12 minutes at 350 degrees F, flipping the fish halfway through.
7. Serve with tartar sauce.

Comfort Classics

BBQ London Broil

2 HOURS 40 MINUTES » MAKES 6 SERVINGS
GET YOUR TASTE BUDS READY FOR A CLASSIC SUNDAY DINNER WITH THIS CAN'T FAIL BEEF DISH KICKED UP WITH HOMEMADE BBQ SAUCE.

2 ½ lbs London broil
¼ cup of your favorite BBQ sauce – OR use the following ingredients to make your own:
2 Tbsp ketchup
2 Tbsp steak sauce
¼ cup apple cider vinegar
1-2 Tbsp Worcestershire sauce
Salt and pepper to taste
1-2 Tbsp molasses (optional)

1. Add your BBQ sauce to a gallon size freezer bag.
2. Using your hands, squeeze the plastic bag to blend the ingredients.
3. Place the meat into the plastic bag and seal it. Be sure the marinade covers the meat. Set the bag on a plate and refrigerate at least 2 to 4 hours.
4. Give the fry basket a coating of non-stick cooking spray.
5. Remove the meat from the plastic bag and place on a plate. Using a paper towel, pat the meat gently to remove excess liquid. Place the steak in the basket and cook on the Steak setting.
6. Flip steak halfway through cooking time.

Classic Mac & Cheese

35 MINUTES » MAKES 4 SERVINGS
AFTER THEY TRY THIS VERSION OF THE HOMESTYLE FAVORITE, YOUR FAMILY WILL NEVER REACH FOR THE BLUE BOX AGAIN.

1 tsp cornstarch
2 cups cheddar cheese, shredded
2 cups macaroni, dry
2 cups heavy whipping cream

1. Mix the cornstarch with 1 ½ cups of the cheese.
2. Once they are combined, add the mixture to a large bowl with the cream and macaroni, reserving the rest of the cheese.
3. Pour into the baking pan and cover with foil. Place into the fry basket and then into the air fryer.
4. Scroll to the Bake setting.
5. Cook for 15 minutes at 310 degrees F.
6. Open and remove foil. Sprinkle the rest of the cheese on top.
7. Place the fry basket back into the air fryer.
8. Scroll to the Bake setting.
9. Cook for 10 minutes at 310 degrees F.

Comfort Classics

Grilled Cheese

10 MINUTES » MAKES 1 SERVING

WE BET YOU THOUGHT THERE WAS NO WAY TO MAKE THE HUMBLE GRILLED CHEESE EVEN BETTER THAN IT WAS BEFORE. BUT YOU NEVER THOUGHT TO AIR FRY IT.

2 slices of your favorite sandwich bread
2-3 slices yellow American or cheddar cheese
2 tsp butter

1. Place cheese between bread slices and butter the outside of each slice.
2. Place in air fryer and cook at 370 degrees F for 8 minutes, flipping halfway through.

Good Ol' Onion Rings

15 MINUTES » MAKES 6 SERVINGS

SURE, FRIES ARE GREAT AND ALL, BUT SOMETIMES THESE TANGY TREATS ARE CALLING YOUR NAME SO LOUD IT DROWNS OUT THE FRENCH FRY'S SONG.

1 bag frozen onion rings
   (Ore-Ida or your favorite)

1. Place onion rings in air fryer basket. Set temperature to 400 degrees F. Cook for 8 minutes for crispy onion rings. Note that you may have to fill your basket in multiple batches to ensure crispiness.
2. Flip contents of basket after 5 minutes, checking to be certain they aren't browning too much. Serve alongside (or as a topping on, we won't judge) your favorite burger or other sandwich.

desserts

Leave room after your delicious air-fried main courses to show off the sweet tooth-sating potential of your new favorite appliance.

Churros
Recipe on page 92

Desserts

Homemade Pop Tarts

25 MINUTES » MAKES 2 SERVINGS

BELIEVE US: THIS DO-IT-YOURSELF VERSION OF THE CORNER STORE CLASSIC IS WORTH THE TIME AND EFFORT.

1 refrigerated or homemade pie crust
½ cup strawberry jam
Cooking spray
½ cup greek yogurt, for icing (optional)

1. Lay out pie crust.
2. Using a cookie cutter, cut out two shapes for every pop tart you want to make.
3. Spoon out about a Tbsp of jam (more or less depending on the size of your cutout) and spread it within ½-inch of your edge.
4. Carefully place the other cutout on top of your jam and gently press edges together using a fork.
5. Place pop tarts in the air fryer, careful that they are not touching. Spray the top of the pop tarts if you want them to crisp a little more, but it's totally not necessary.
6. Cook 7 to 10 minutes on 370 degrees F, checking every minute after 6 minutes for desired doneness.
7. They are ready and delicious at that point, but if you want some healthier "icing," mix a dollop of fruit spread and a dollop of greek yogurt and drizzle over the top!

Churros

35 MINUTES » MAKES 3 SERVINGS

YOU LOVE THE DEEP FRIED VERSION ON SPECIAL OCCASIONS, AND NOW YOU CAN ENJOY THE AIR-FRIED VERSION AT HOME—HOLD THE GUILT.

6 Tbsp unsalted butter
2 ¼ cups water
1 tsp salt
1 tsp vanilla extract
2 ¼ cups all-purpose flour
1 large egg
1 cup sugar
2 tsp ground cinnamon

1. In a medium saucepan over medium-high heat, melt butter then add water, salt and vanilla. Bring to a boil and remove from the heat.
2. Add the flour and stir the mixture with a wooden spoon until a smooth dough is formed. (It should be almost like the texture of homemade play dough.)
3. Let the dough cool for about 15 minutes then transfer to a bowl and add the egg. Stir quickly until egg is mixed in.
4. Transfer dough to a piping bag fitted with a 1M tip.
5. Pipe several 6-inch sticks of churro dough into the air fryer making sure they don't touch.
6. Bake at 380 degrees F for 10 minutes.
7. While the churros are cooking you can make the cinnamon sugar mixture by combining the two in a bowl and mixing. Sprinkle over cooked churros and serve.

Apple Pie

30 MINUTES » MAKES 2 SERVINGS

AS AMERICAN AS BASEBALL AND JAZZ, THIS DESSERT WILL KEEP THEM COMING BACK FOR MORE, À LA MODE OR NOT.

1 red apple
1 green apple
1 Tbsp cinnamon
3 Tbsp white sugar
3 Tbsp brown sugar
1 Tbsp apple cider vinegar
1 cup flour
½ Tbsp sugar
½ tsp salt
3 Tbsp butter
3 Tbsp lard or shortening
3-4 Tbsp ice water

1. Chop your apples into tiny pieces and combine all filling ingredients through the vinegar together in a large bowl. Set aside to let the flavor develop.
2. To make your pie crust, mix the flour, sugar, salt, butter and shortening together with a fork or your hands.
3. Add 3 Tbsp of water and knead, adding more to get a cohesive dough.
4. Roll out your pie crust to a ½-inch thickness and then cut into your desired pie shapes.
5. Spoon one tablespoon of the filling into the center of half of the pie shapes, and then place a second pie crust shape overtop. Press around the edges to seal.
6. Place in the air fryer and add oil to the dispenser.
7. Bake at 360 degrees F for 7 to 10 minutes, watching carefully.

Tasty Cupcakes

40 MINUTES » MAKES 2 SERVINGS

SURE, THERE'S ALWAYS THAT $10 CUPCAKE THE SIZE OF YOUR HEAD: BUT THESE ARE BETTER FOR YOU, AND COME WITH THE BENEFIT OF BEING CLOSER TO ALL YOUR STUFF.

3 ½ oz caster sugar
¾ tsp baking powder
2 eggs
3 drops vanilla essence
3.5 oz softened butter or margarine
3.5 oz self-raising flour

1. Place all the ingredients into a bowl and use a hand mixer to whisk all the ingredients together until light and creamy.
2. Fill your silicone cupcake molds half full of the mixture.
3. Place the cakes inside the fry basket. Set the timer for 20 minutes and cook at 350 degrees F.
4. Keep an eye on them for over browning and check if they're cooked by pressing one gently: if it rises back up it is cooked.
5. Once cooked, carefully remove the interval and place it onto roasting rack to cool. After five minutes remove the cakes from the inner bowl and cool them for a further 15 minutes on a roasting rack before decorating.

Desserts

Peach Hand Pies

30 MINUTES » MAKES 3 SERVINGS

YOU DON'T NEED A FRONT PORCH, ROCKING CHAIR OR TALL GLASS OF SWEET TEA TO ENJOY THESE PIES, BUT IT CERTAINLY DOES PUT YOU IN A FINE MOOD.

2 (5-oz) fresh peaches, peeled and chopped
1 Tbsp fresh lemon juice (from 1 lemon)
3 Tbsp granulated sugar
1 tsp vanilla extract
¼ tsp table salt
1 tsp cornstarch
1 (14.1-oz) pkg. refrigerated pie crusts
Cooking spray

1. Stir together peaches, lemon juice, sugar, vanilla and salt in a medium bowl. Let stand 15 minutes, stirring occasionally. Drain peaches, reserving 1 Tbsp liquid. Whisk cornstarch into reserved liquid; stir into drained peaches.
2. Cut pie crusts into 8 (4-inch) circles. Place about a Tbsp filling in center of each circle. Brush edges of dough with water; fold dough over filling to form half-moons. Crimp edges with a fork to seal; cut 3 small slits in top of pies. Coat pies well with cooking spray.
3. Place 3 pies in a single layer in the air fryer basket, and cook at 350 degrees F until golden brown, 12 to 14 minutes. Repeat with remaining pies.

Chocolate Cake

40 MINUTES » MAKES 2 SERVINGS

EVEN YOUR PICKIEST GUESTS WILL AGREE THIS DESSERT IS A HIT NO MATTER WHEN IT'S SERVED.

3 eggs
½ cup sour cream
1 cup flour
⅔ cup sugar
1 stick butter, room temperature
⅓ cup cocoa powder
1 tsp baking powder
½ tsp baking soda
2 tsp vanilla

1. Preheat air fryer to 320 degrees F
2. Mix ingredients in a stand mixer on low.
3. Pour into cake carrel.
4. Place in the air fryer basket and cook for 25 minutes.
5. Once timer rings, use a toothpick to see if cake is done.
6. Cool cake on a wire rack.
7. Ice with your favorite frosting.

Small-Batch Brownies

35 MINUTES » MAKES 2 SERVINGS

AFTER ONE TASTE OF THESE AIR-FRYER PHENOMS, EVERYONE WILL BE CALLING THESE YOUR "SPECIAL BROWNIES."

WET INGREDIENTS
¼ cup non dairy milk
¼ cup aquafaba
½ tsp vanilla extract

DRY INGREDIENTS
½ cup whole wheat pastry flour
 (*use gluten-free baking blend)
½ cup vegan sugar
 (or sweetener of choice, to taste)
¼ cup cocoa powder
1 Tbsp ground flax seeds
¼ tsp salt

MIX-INS
¼ cup of any one or a combination of the following: chopped walnuts, hazelnuts, pecans, mini vegan chocolate chips, shredded coconut

1. Mix the dry ingredients together in one bowl. Then mix the wet ingredients in a large measuring cup. Add the wet to the dry and mix well.
2. Add in the mix-in(s) of your choice and mix again.
3. Preheat your air fryer to 350 degrees F. Either spray some oil on a 5-inch cake or pie round pan (or a loaf pan that fits in your air fryer), or line it with parchment paper to keep it completely oil-free.
4. Place the pan in the fryer basket. Cook for 20 minutes on Bake setting. If the middle is not well set or a knife doesn't come out clean when stuck in the middle cook for 5 minutes more and repeat as needed.

Cinnamon Donut Bites

40 MINUTES » MAKES 3 SERVINGS

EVER WANT A WHOLE DONUT BUT ALSO WANT TO SAVE SOME ROOM FOR OTHER PARTY SNACKS? YOU'RE IN LUCK. BEHOLD: HOMEMADE DONUT HOLES.

⅔ cup all-purpose flour
⅔ cup whole-wheat flour
2 Tbsp granulated sugar
1 tsp baking powder
¼ tsp ground cinnamon
¼ tsp kosher salt
4 Tbsp cold salted butter, cut into small pieces
⅓ cup whole milk
Cooking spray
2 cups (about 8 oz.) powdered sugar
3 Tbsp water

1. Whisk together flours, granulated sugar, baking powder, cinnamon and salt.
2. Add butter; cut into mixture using 2 knives or a pastry cutter until butter is well combined with flour and mixture resembles coarse cornmeal. Add milk and stir together until dough forms a ball. Place dough on a floured surface and knead until dough is smooth and forms a cohesive ball, about 30 seconds. Cut dough into 16 equal pieces. Gently roll each piece into a smooth ball.
3. Coat air fryer basket well with cooking spray. Place 8 balls in the fryer basket, leaving room between each.
4. Spray donut balls with cooking spray. Cook at 350 degrees F until browned and puffed, 10 to 12 minutes. Gently remove donut balls from basket, and place on a wire rack over foil. Let cool 5 minutes. Repeat with remaining donut balls.
5. Whisk together powdered sugar and water in a medium bowl until smooth. Gently spoon half of the glaze over donut balls. Let cool.

Index

A
Apple, 40
   green, 93
   red, 93
Aquafaba, 95
Avocado(s), 16
   oil, 29, 30, 36

B
Bacon, 20, 25
Baking powder, 15, 16, 93, 94, 95
Baking soda, 94
Bananas, 44
Beef
   baby back ribs, 56
   corned, 61
   ground, 53, 54, 71
   London broil, 86
   mincemeat, 71
   rib eye steak, 51
   strip steak, 62
Beets, 39
Blueberries, 36
Bread
   hot dog buns, 36
   pita, 46
   sandwich, 89
   stale, 54
Breadcrumbs, 15, 23, 26, 30, 35, 54, 67, 72, 81
   panko, 16, 35, 64, 81, 85
Broccoli florets, 59
Brown sugar, 36, 93
Brussels sprouts, 29
Buttermilk, 64

C
Carrots, 26
Cauliflower, riced, 68
Celery, 72
Cheese, 36
   American, 89
   cheddar, 15, 20, 23, 25, 82, 86, 89
   feta, 43
   Fontina, 23
   Gruyere, 23
   Mexican, 59
   mozzarella, 46, 68, 85
   Parmesan, 15, 20, 23, 29, 35, 46, 54, 72, 82
   Swiss, 61
Chicken
   fajita strips, frozen, 59
   thighs, 61
   wings, 39, 40, 79
Chickpeas, 43
Chocolate chips, vegan, 95
Cocoa powder, 62, 94, 95
Coconut
   oil, 64
   shredded, 95
Cod, 85
Corn, 19, 25
Cornflakes, 81
Cornish hen, 64
Cornstarch, 86, 94
Crackers, dried prawn, 44

D
Dip, Dean's Bacon Cheddar, 25
Dressing, Thousand Island salad, 61

E
Eggplant, 46
Empanada disks (Goya), 56

F
Flaxseed, 71, 95
Flour
   chickpea, 19
   seasoned, 64
   self-rising, 36, 93
   wheat pastry, 95

G
Garlic puree, 26
Ghee, 26
Ginger, 72
Green beans, 29

H
Hazelnuts, 95
Heavy cream, 23, 36, 86
Herbs
   chives, 20, 25, 82
   cilantro, 61
   dill, 35
   mint, 26
   parsley, 20, 54, 82
Honey, 26, 44

J
Jam, strawberry, 92

K
Ketchup, 16, 19, 86

L
Lard, 93
Lemon(s), 39, 61, 72
   juice, 29, 36, 94
Liquid smoke, 53, 62, 71

M
Mayonnaise, canola, 16
Molasses, 86

Monk fruit, 36
Mustard
   coarse-ground, 82
   yellow, 81

O
Okra, 30
Onions, 26, 59, 64, 72
   red, 61
   spring, 82
Onion rings, frozen, 89
Oysters, 81

P
Panko, *see Breadcrumbs*
Pasta, 23
   macaroni, 86
Peaches, 94
Pecans, 95
Peppers
   bell, 82
   green, 59, 61
   green chile, 72
Phyllo shells, 43
Picadillo, 56
Pickle, dill, 35
Pie crust, 92, 94
Pizza
   crust, 61
   dough, 20
   toppings, 68
Plantains, 30
Pollock, 67
Potato(es), 19, 25, 72
   mashed, 15
   red, 15, 59
   Russet, 19
   starch, 39
   yukon gold, 20
Psyllium powder, 68

S
Salsa, 59
Salmon, 64
Sauce
   BBQ, 56, 86
   buffalo, 79
   hot, 81
   Maggi seasoning, 53
   marinara, 20, 46
   soy, 59, 62
   spaghetti, 71
   Sriracha chili, 16
   steak, 86
   tartar, 85
   Worcestershire, 53, 86
   yogurt tahini, 19
Sauerkraut, 61
Sausage, 26
   breakfast patty, 82
   hot dogs, 36, 81
   pork, 82
Shrimp, 72
Sour cream, 20, 59, 94
Spices
   basil, 15, 40, 72
   cinnamon, 40, 92, 93, 95
   Cajun seasoning, 81
   cayenne pepper, 35, 40, 61
   chaat masala, 44
   chili flakes, 26
   coriander, 43
   Creole seasoning, 81
   cumin, 43
   curry powder, 61
   dill weed, 64
   Emeril's original essence, 23
   Flavor God Garlic Lovers seasoning, 68
   Garam Masala, 61
   garlic powder, 15, 26, 35, 40, 43, 53, 59
   garlic salt, 35, 46
   ginger, 43
   Italian seasoning, 15, 35, 46
   McCormick's Grill Mates Montreal Steak seasoning, 62, 71
   nutmeg, 23, 82
   Old Bay seasoning, 39
   onion powder, 40, 53, 59, 72
   oregano, 40, 54, 72
   paprika, 40
      smoked, 61
   parsley, 53
   sage, 26
   steak rub, 51, 62
   thyme, 40
   True Lemon seasoning, 39
   turmeric powder, 44, 59
   white pepper, 40
Spinach, frozen, 43

T
Taco shells, 59
Tofu, 59
Tortillas, corn, 13
Tuna, albacore, 72
Turkey breast, 53

V
Vanilla
   essence, 93, 94
   extract, 36, 92, 94, 95
Vegan sugar, 95
Vinegar
   apple cider, 16, 86, 93

W
Walnuts, 95
Wheat germ, 46

Y
Yogurt, Greek, 61, 92

Z
Zucchini, 19, 35, 71

A Topix Media Lab Publication
For inquiries, call 646-476-8860

CEO Tony Romando

Senior Vice President of Sales & New Markets Tom Mifsud
Vice President of Retail Sales & Logistics Linda Greenblatt
Director of Finance Vandana Patel
Manufacturing Director Nancy Puskuldjian
Financial Analyst Matthew Quinn
Brand Marketing & Promotions Assistant Emily McBride

Chief Content Officer Jeff Ashworth
Director of Editorial Operations Courtney Kerrigan
Creative Director Steven Charny
Photo Director Dave Weiss

Issue Editor Tim Baker
Art Director Susan Dazzo
Senior Editor Trevor Courneen
Associate Editor Juliana Sharaf
Designer Kelsey Payne
Copy Editor & Fact Checker Tara Sherman

Co-Founders Bob Lee, Tony Romando

Topix Media Lab Special #1, 2020. The Ultimate Air Fryer Handbook published by Topix Media Lab, 14 Wall Street, Suite 4B, New York, NY 10005. All rights reserved. No material in this issue may be reprinted without the written permission of the publisher. Entire contents copyright © 2020. Certain photographs used in this publication are used by license or permission from the owner thereof, or are otherwise publicly available. This publication is not endorsed by any person or entity appearing herein. Any product names, logos, brands or other trademarks featured or referred to in the publication are the property of their respective trademark owners. Topix Media Lab is not affiliated with, nor sponsored or endorsed by, any of the persons, entities, product names, logos, brands or other trademarks featured or referred to in any of its publications. PRINTED IN THE USA.

Note to our readers
The information in this magazine should not be substituted for, or used to alter, medical therapy without your doctor's advice. For a specific health problem, consult your physician for guidance.

The information in this magazine has been carefully researched, and every reasonable effort has been made to ensure its accuracy. Neither the magazine's publisher nor its creators assume any responsibility for any accidents, injuries, losses or other damages that might come from its use. You are solely responsible for taking any and all reasonable and necessary precautions when performing the activities detailed in its pages.

Recipes supplied by Yedi Houseware Appliances

All photos: Shutterstock except:
2 Jeremy Pawlowski/Stocksy; 14 Brent Hofacker/Alamy; 21 Anjelika Gretskaia/Alamy; 37 Daniel Hurst/Stocksy; 46 Cultura Creative/Alamy; 58 David Cabrera Navarro/Alamy; 73 Brent Hofacker/Alamy

Indexing by R studio T, NYC

ISBN: 9781948174718

Go to OnNewsstandsNow.com
for back issues of our
Special Editions

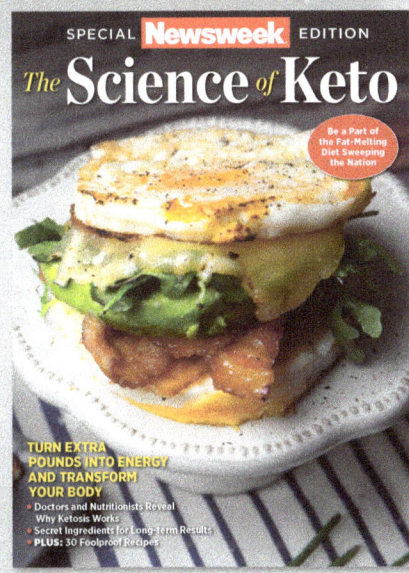

Plus the latest issues BEFORE they hit stores!

www.ingramcontent.com/pod-product-compliance
Lightning Source LLC
Chambersburg PA
CBHW051348110526
44591CB00025B/2945